What We Have in Common

A Brim Coloring Book

Written by Jane Landey
Edited by David Austin

Drawings by David Austin and Jane Austin

Introduction

What We Have in Common. Brim Coloring Books enables children to color the drawings as they read along. In this series the ostrich and the emu are compared. The facts enable children to appreciate common values. Thus, imbibing in them interest towards animals which could help them appreciate what they have in common with one another.

The ostrich and the emu have many things in common. They look alike and run very fast. They are the largest birds in the world. Both of them live in the forest.

THE OSTRICH

AND

THE EMU

The ostrich and the emu meet on
a green grassy field.

I am an ostrich Mister Emu.

I am an emu Mister Ostrich.

I have a long neck.

I have a long neck too!

I have long legs.

I have long legs too!

My webs are thick.

I have thick webs too!

My body is big!

My body is big too!

My beak is long!

My beak is long too!

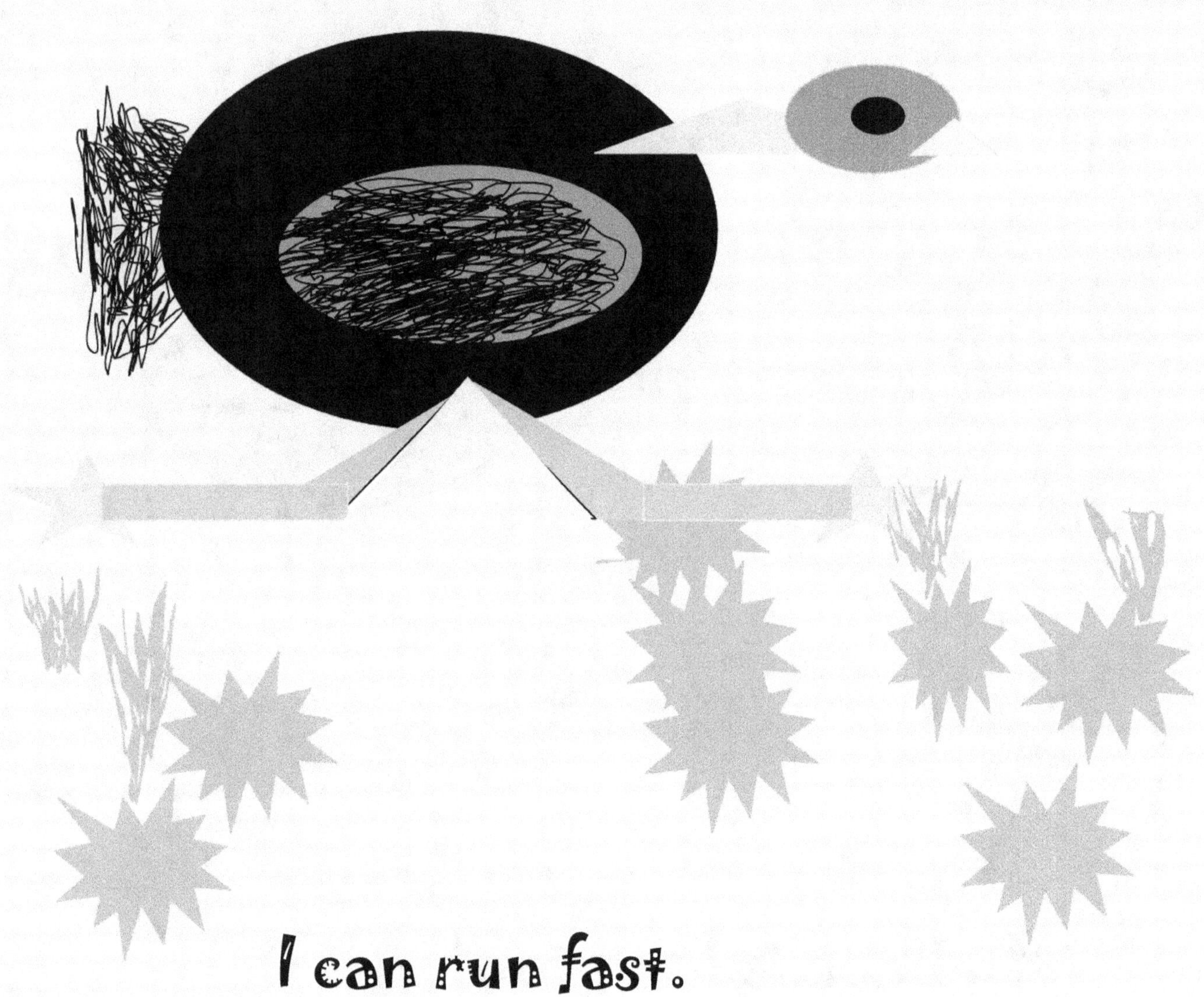

I can run fast.

I can run fast too.

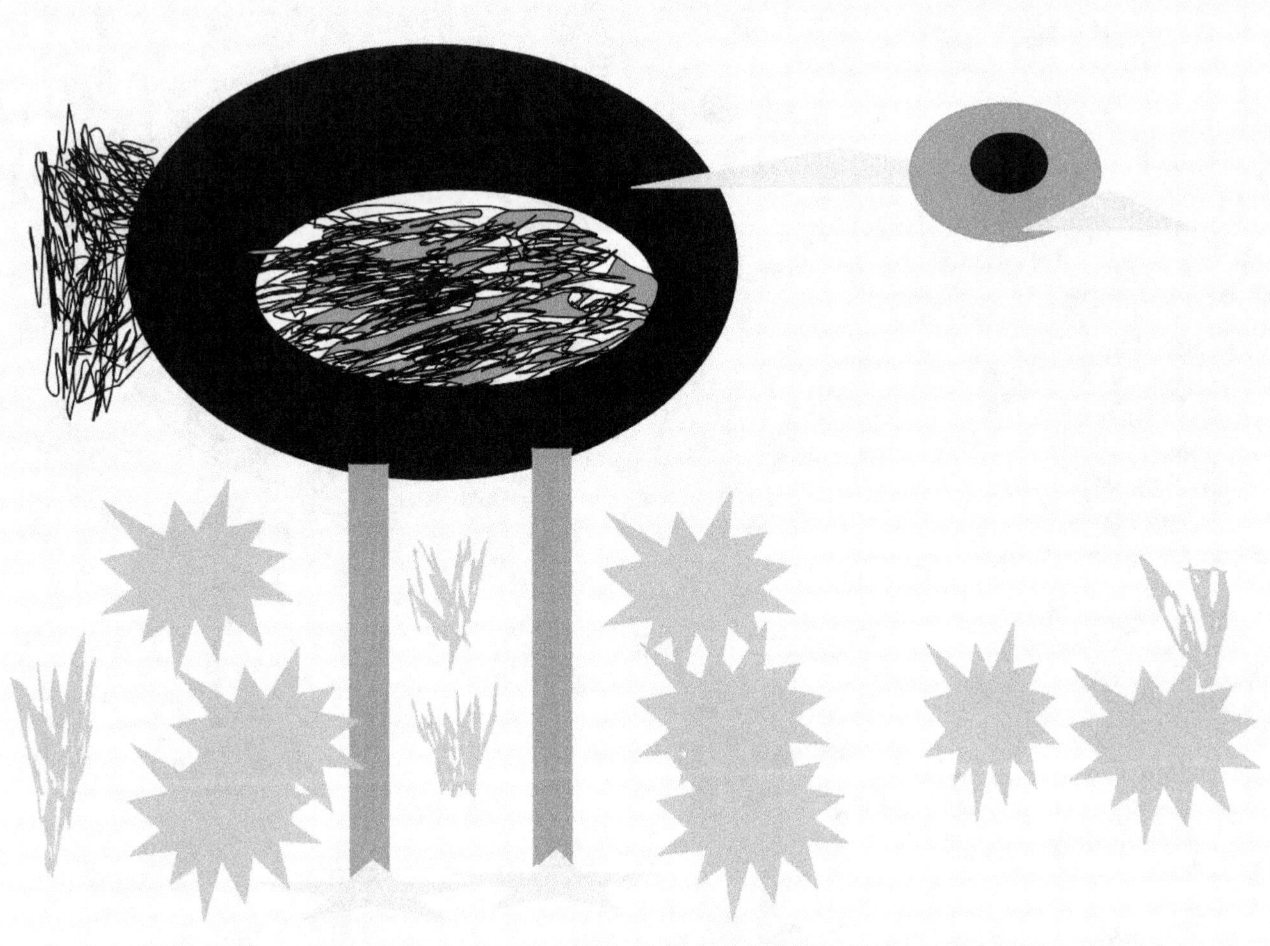

My head has a few hairs!

My head has a few hairs too!

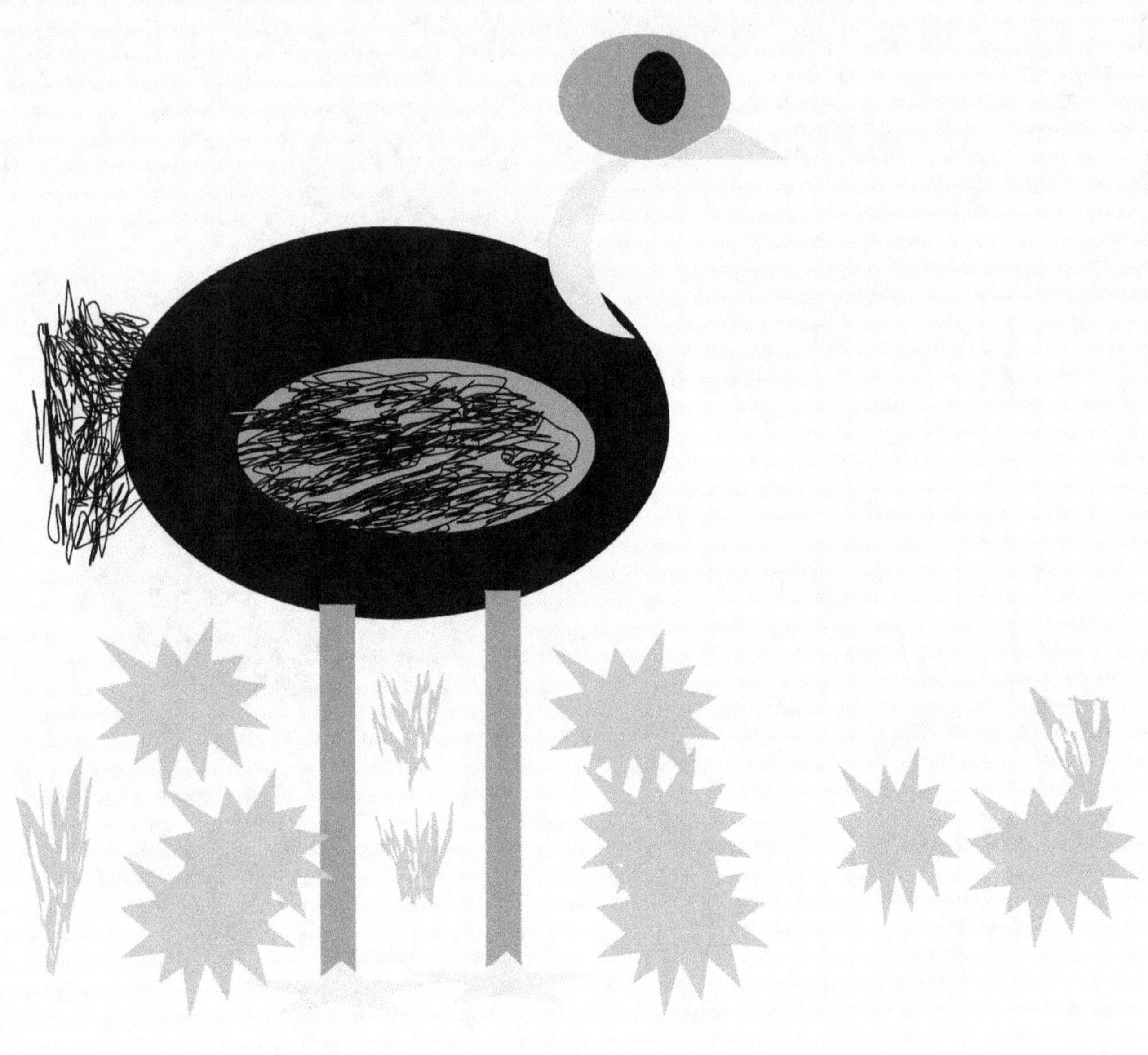

My feathers are dark. I can
say black!

My feathers are dark too. I can
say brownish!

I am the largest bird in the world!

I am the second largest bird in the world!

An ostrich has few feathers and cannot fly.

An emu has few feathers and
cannot fly either!

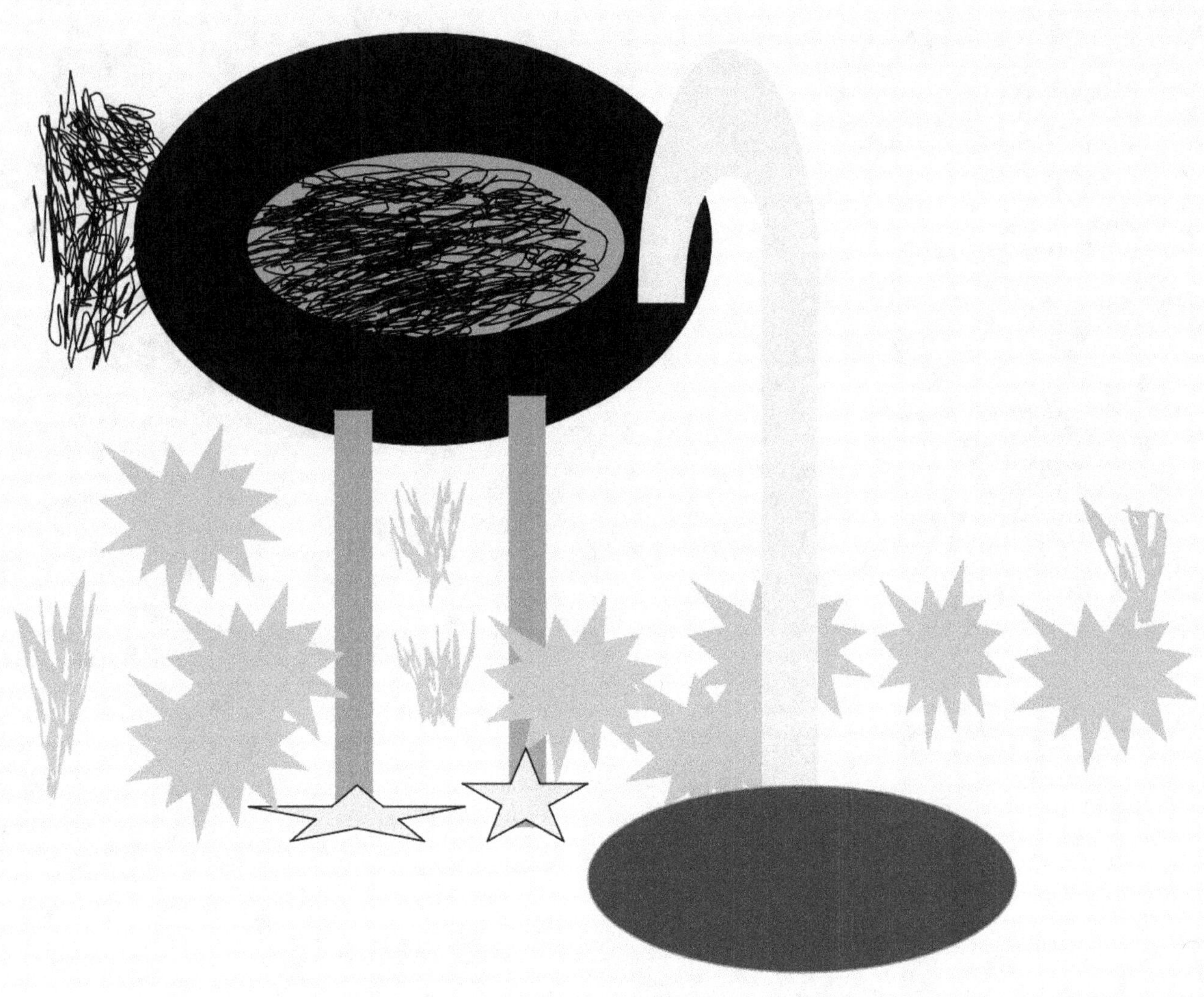

As an ostrich I can bury my head in the soil.

As an emu I can bury my head in the soil too!

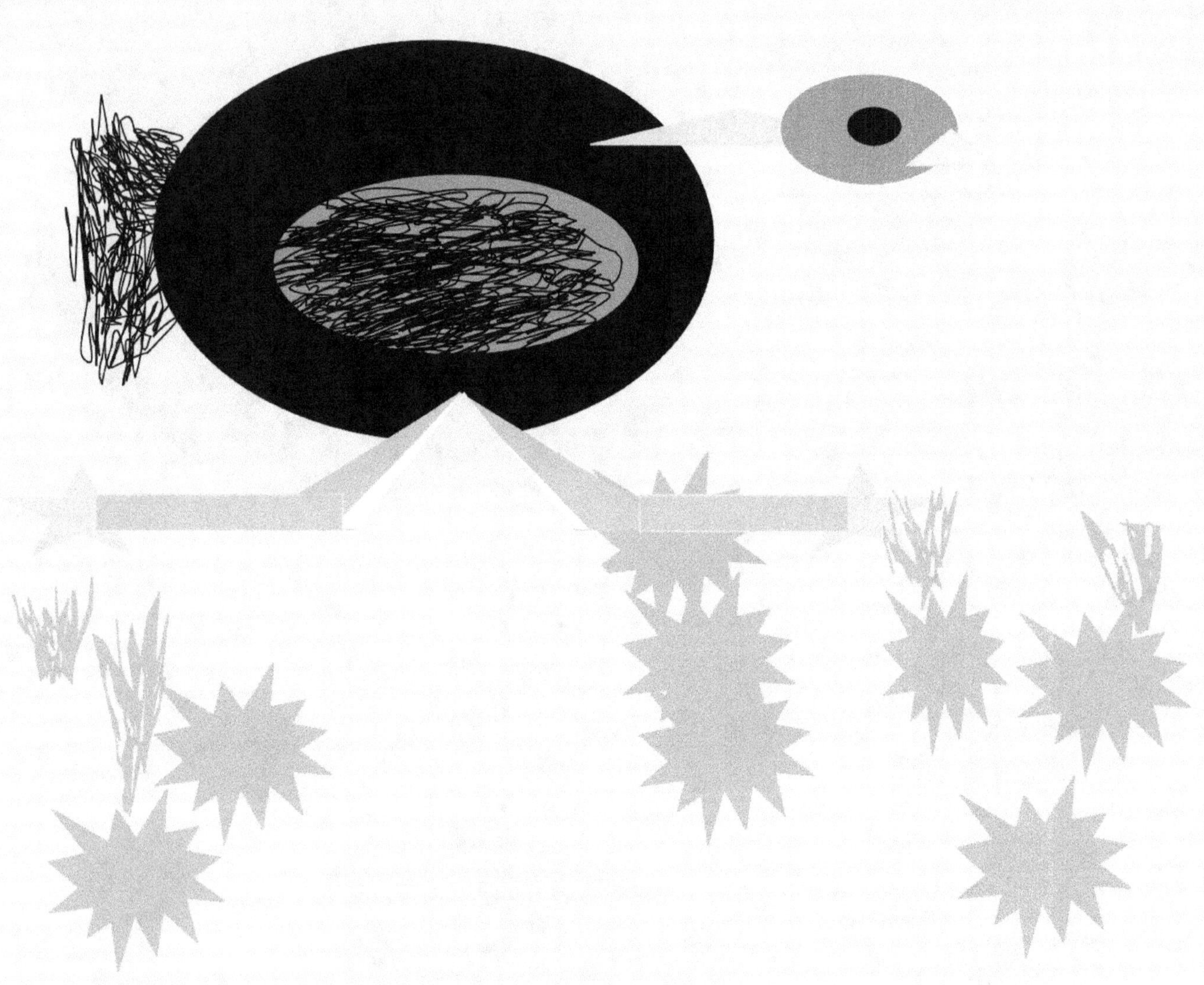

Ostrich legs are long enough to carry its body.

Emu has long legs that carry its body too!

I have long legs Mister Emu.

I have long legs too Mister
Ostrich!

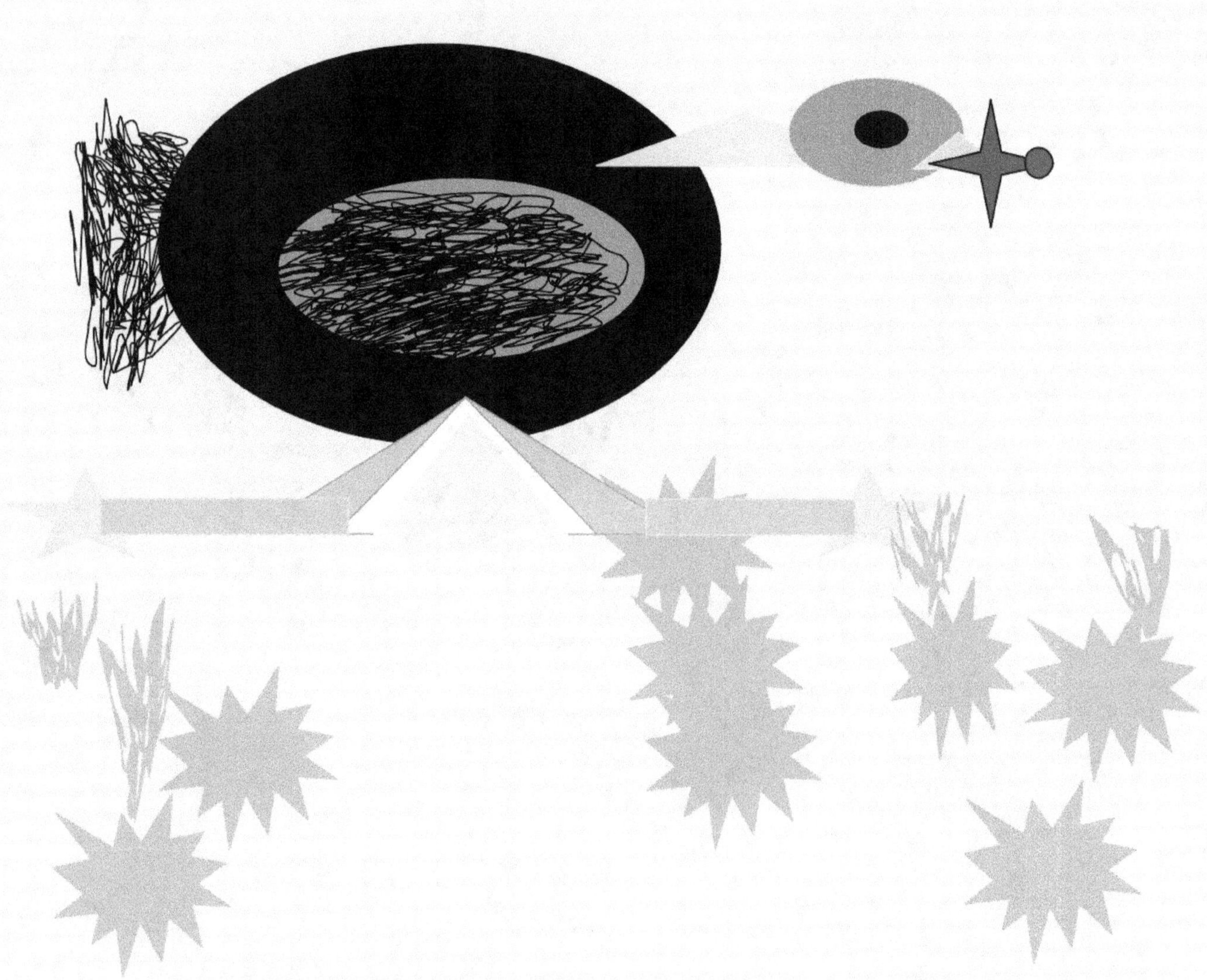

I can catch a fly with my beak.

I can catch a fly with my beak too!

Who is taller, you or me?

I know I am Mister Emu!

What We Have in Common Brim Coloring Books
Crocodile and Alligator
Turtle and Tortoise
Starfish and Octopus
Worm and Snake
Turkey and Vulture
Ostrich and Emu
Weka and Kiwi
Bat and Rat
Camel and Llama
Duck and Pelican
Kangaroo and Wallaby
Pig and Tapir
Skunk and Squirrel
Hedge and Anteater
Cat and Owl
Elephant and Rhinoceros
Dog and fox
Buffalo and Bull
Leopard and Cheetah
Horse and Zebra

www.ingramcontent.com/pod-product-compliance
Lightning Source LLC
Chambersburg PA
CBHW081254250726
48654CB00012B/1609